GERMAN CAMPS IN POLAND

POLISH HISTORY DURING WORLD WAR 2

PIOTR LEWICKI

Copyright © 2017. All Rights Reserved.

No part of this publication may be reproduced, distributed, or transmitted in any form or by any means, including photocopying, recording, or other electronic or mechanical methods, or by any information storage and retrieval system without the prior written permission of the publisher, except in the case of very brief quotations embodied in critical reviews and certain other noncommercial uses permitted by copyright law.

Why You Should Read This Book

Concentration camps and extermination centers were established and administered by the German state. At the time when those camps were being established, the state of Poland did not exist. The area of Auschwitz was not only occupied by Germany but also incorporated geographically into the German state. During the German occupation of Poland (1939-1945) the legally operating center of Polish authorities was the Government of the Republic of Poland in exile situated in London, who neither made decisions concerning the establishing of those concentration camps nor participated in any manner in their administration. The structures of the Polish underground state, which were subordinated to the Polish Government in exile, did not participate in any manner in operating those camps, either, and undertook actions aimed against their German initiators and managers.

Despite the semantic ambiguity of the term "Polish concentration camps", its solely acceptable geographic connotation is only obvious for a relatively small number of people who are familiar with the history of Europe and the Second World War.

This book will enlight you on the polish history of the camps so you can be confedent enough about the real fact, and stop following the masses.

Table of Contents

Auschwitz-Birkenau Camp 6

"Polish Death Camps" this words can lead you to jail in Poland 11

Treblinka Camp 15

Bełżec Camp 15

Majdanek Camp 16

Chełmno Camp 18

Sobibór Camp 18

Dachau Camp 19

Mauthausen-Gusen Camp 20

Bergen-Belsen Camp 21

Buchenwald Camp 22

Conclusion 23

about The Author 26

In 1933, the first Nazi concentration camp was built in Dachau, Germany to imprison dissidents. Heinrich Himmler took over in 1934 and start arresting "racially undesirable elements" – Jews, Gypsies, Jehovah's Witnesses, homosexuals, and the (mentally) disabled.

Germany invaded Poland in 1939, and since Poland had a vast Jewish population, more camps were built. The killings began in 1941, and the following year, Germany started to exterminate the undesirables in staggering numbers.

As WWII progressed, more camps were built for different purposes. There were those for POWs, those for slave labor, and those designed for extermination. The following were the worst in terms of casualty rates.

AUSCHWITZ-BIRKENAU CAMP

Train tracks leading to the "Gate of Death," the main entrance of Auschwitz II

Built in Poland it was actually a vast network of 48 sites. Also called Auschwitz I, II, and III for the main facilities, they had 45 other satellite camps. Auschwitz I originally held Polish political prisoners who were first sent there in May 1940. It was at Auschwitz II (Birkenau), where the exterminations began in 1942.

Of those killed some 90% were Jewish, the rest were Poles, Soviets, Romani, Sinti, Jehovah's Witnesses, gays, and those of mixed German blood. Though gassing was a major cause of death, so was overwork, malnutrition, poor conditions, inhumane treatment, and infectious diseases.

Auschwitz, Polish Oświęcim, also called Auschwitz-Birkenau, Nazi Germany's largest concentration camp and extermination camp. Located near the industrial town of Oświęcim in southern Poland (in a portion of the country that was annexed by Germany at the beginning of World War II), Auschwitz was actually three camps in one: a prison camp, an extermination camp, and a slave-labour camp. As the most lethal of the Nazi extermination camps, Auschwitz has become the emblematic site of the "final solution," a virtual synonym for the Holocaust. Between 1.1 and 1.5 million people died at Auschwitz; 90 percent of them were Jews. Also among the dead were some 19,000 Roma who were held at the camp until the Nazis gassed them on July 31,

1944—the only other victim group gassed in family units alongside the Jews. The Poles constituted the second largest victim group at Auschwitz, where some 83,000 were killed or died.

The entrance gates to the Auschwitz concentration camp, near Kraków, Poland; the sign reads "Arbeit Macht Frei" ("Work Liberates").

Auschwitz

Auschwitz was probably chosen to play a central role in the "final solution" because it was located at a railway junction with 44 parallel tracks—rail lines that were used to transport Jews from throughout Europe to their death. Heinrich Himmler, chief of the SS, the Nazi paramilitary corps, ordered the establishment of the first camp, the prison camp, on April 27, 1940, and the first transport of Polish political prisoners arrived on June 14. This small camp, Auschwitz I, was reserved throughout its history for political prisoners, mainly Poles and Germans.

In October 1941, work began on Auschwitz II, or Birkenau, located outside the nearby village of Brzezinka. There the SS later developed a huge concentration camp and extermination complex that included some 300 prison barracks; four large so-called Badeanstalten (German: "bathhouses"), in which prisoners were gassed to death; Leichenkeller ("corpse cellars"), in which their bodies were stored; and Einäscherungsöfen ("cremating ovens"). Another camp (Buna-Monowitz), near the village of Dwory, later called Auschwitz III, became in May 1942 a slave-labour camp supplying workers for the nearby chemical and synthetic-rubber works of IG Farben. In addition, Auschwitz became the nexus of a complex of 45 smaller subcamps in the region, most of which housed slave labourers. During most of the period from 1940 to 1945, the commandant of the central Auschwitz camps was SS-Hauptsturmführer (Captain) Rudolf Franz Höss.

The death camp and slave-labour camp were interrelated. Newly arrived prisoners at the death camp were divided in a process known as Selektion. The young and the able-bodied were sent to work. Young children and their mothers and the old and infirm were sent directly to the gas chambers. Thousands of prisoners were also selected by the camp doctor, Josef Mengele, for medical experiments. Auschwitz doctors tested methods of sterilization on the prisoners, using massive doses of radiation, uterine injections, and other barbaric procedures. Experiments involving the killing of twins, upon whom autopsies were performed, were meant to provide information that would supposedly lead to the rapid expansion of the "Aryan race."

Matsya avatar of Vishnu, 19th-century lithograph. Vishnu in his avatar of Matsya, a fish. Lithograph from L'Inde Francaise, Paris, 1828. Hindu trinity, Hinduism. World Religions: Fact or Fiction?

Subject to harsh conditions—including inadequate shelter and sanitation—given minimal food, and worked to exhaustion, those who could no longer work faced transport back to Birkenau for gassing. German corporations invested heavily in the slave-labour industries adjacent to Auschwitz. In 1942 IG Farben alone invested more than 700 million Reichsmarks in its facilities at Auschwitz III.

Between May 15 and July 9, 1944, some 438,000 Hungarian Jews were shipped on 147 trains to Birkenau, stretching the camp's resources for killing beyond all limits. Because the crematoria were overcrowded, bodies were burned in pyres fueled partly by the victims' own fat. Just prior to the deportation of Hungarian Jewry, two prisoners escaped with plans of the camp. They met with resistance leaders in Slovakia and compiled a detailed report including maps. As this report made its way to Western intelligence services in the summer of 1944, there were requests to bomb Auschwitz. Although the industrial complex adjacent to Auschwitz was bombed, the death camp and its crematoria were left untouched, a subject of controversy more than 50 years later

As Soviet armies advanced in 1944 and early 1945, Auschwitz was gradually abandoned. On January 18, 1945, some 60,000 prisoners were marched to Wodzisław Śląski, where they were put on freight trains (many in open cars) and sent westward to concentration camps away from the front. One in four died on the road from starvation, cold, exhaustion, and despair. Many were shot along the way in what became known as the "death marches." The 7,650 sick or starving prisoners who remained were found by arriving Soviet troops on January 27, 1945.

Although the Germans destroyed parts of the camps before abandoning them in 1945, much of Auschwitz I and Auschwitz II (Birkenau) remained intact and were later converted into a museum and memorial. The site has been threatened by increased industrial activity in Oświęcim. In 1996, however, the Polish government joined with other organizations in a large-scale effort to ensure its preservation. Originally named Auschwitz Concentration Camp, the memorial was designated a UNESCO World Heritage site in 1979. It was renamed "Auschwitz-Birkenau. The Nazi German Concentration and Extermination Camp (1940–1945)" in 2007.

"POLISH DEATH CAMPS" THIS WORDS CAN LEAD YOU TO JAIL IN POLAND

It's been almost 77 years since Nazi Germany invaded Poland, which sparked the official beginning of World War II. Nearly 18 percent of Poland's population were murdered during the Nazi occupation—at least 4.9 million people, three million of whom were Jews. Decades after the war ended, the sites of concentration camps including Auschwitz-Birkenau and Treblinka stand as monuments to the terror of the Holocaust and the Polish government cares so deeply about how people refer to the true origins of the camps that they just passed a law that threatens those who refer to the camps as "Polish" with up to three years in prison. But is the attempt to outlaw terms like "Polish death camps" a bid for historical accuracy—or an attempt to whitewash history?

The AP reports that a new bill will dole out prison terms for people who refer to Nazi death camps as "Polish." Phrases like "Polish death camps" and "Polish concentration camps" will be punished by the law, which is expected to pass in the Polish parliament soon, and be implemented later this year. The punishment—which includes fines or up to three years jail time and applies to everyone, even those who use the term unintentionally—is actually less harsh than the five-year sentences originally recommended by advocates.

The topic is a sensitive one to the Polish government, as President Obama learned in 2012 when he used the term "Polish death camp" during a posthumous Presidential Medal of Freedom ceremony for Polish resistance fighter Jan Karski. Throughout the German occupation of Poland, Karski smuggled information about Nazi activities to the Polish government in exile and tried to sound the alarm on the Holocaust after witnessing the treatment of Polish Jews in the Warsaw Ghetto and what seems to have been a transit camp funneling Jews to the Bełżec extermination camp.

The diplomatic drama that resulted from Obama's mistake culminated in letters from the Polish president asking for him to officially correct his statement. Obama wrote back: "I regret the error and agree that this moment is an opportunity to ensure that this and future generations know the truth."

The Polish Embassy itself maintains an ongoing list of "interventions" against the term and even has a how-to guide for readers who want to help eliminate the term. The embassy's public campaign resulted in updates to several journalistic style guides, from the AP, which instructs journalists not to "confuse the location and the perpetrators," to the New York Times, whose style guide advises journalists to "take extra care" due to the sensitivity of the topic.

But what may initially seem like an attempt to report on history more accurately is complicated by the context around it. The new law comes in the wake of new government controls on the Polish media and the election of a right-wing, nativist party. As Marc Herman writes for The Columbia Journalism Review, the recent "media grab" has prompted high-profile journalists to resign, puts the Polish government in charge of hiring and firing, and has led to a more nationalist media climate in the country.

It's been coming to this for a while: In 2012, Tablet Magazine's Michael Moynihan noted an ongoing Polish media trend that favors heroic Polish narratives while overlooking the Nazi collaboration and anti-Semitism that occurred within Poland during the Nazi occupation. Polish nationalists, writes Moynihan, prefer a "black-and-white morality tale starring heroic Poles who acted righteously under Nazi domination" instead of a more nuanced portrayal of a horrific part of Poland's past.

The legacy of Poland during the Holocaust is complex. Though the Nazis undeniably were behind the concentration camps that dotted occupied Poland, everyday Poles did participate in the horrors of World War II, participating in pogroms, denouncing and blackmailing Jews, and participating in some death camps. At the same time, Poland organized one of Europe's biggest resistance movements, and many Poles who were not a part of the organized resistance helped and even saved their Jewish neighbors.

Is Poland trying to set the record straight or detract attention from its own uncomfortable legacy? Is it historically accurate or just whitewashing to favor narratives of Polish resistance to the Nazis over the rampant anti-Semitism that played out within occupied Poland during the war?

You be the judge. Just don't say the words "Polish death camps" while you do it—you could be headed to jail.

Not too many people know what happened in Auschwitz. Least of us might think, that it was the largest Nazi Germany's concentration and extermination camps, created in Nazi German occupied Poland. thousands of people died there and we all should learn a lesson with this story.

Firstly, all what is said about Auschwitz is real. You can heat some rumors, that that camp was a scam of some kind, but statistics don't lie. The camp commandant, Rudolf Hoss, testified that up to 3 million people had lost their lives at Auschwitz. Most of them were killed in deadly gas chambers using "Zyklon B". The rest died because of starvation, forced labour and lack of disease control.

The exact number of people who died in Auschwitz is still unknown. The Nazis destroyed most of records, therefore we will never be certain. German officers claimed it might be a number below 2 million people. Communist Polish and Soviet authorities on the contrary estimate that number to be between 2,5 and 4 million.

No matter what the number is, one thing is certain - an unimaginable tragedy had happened there

TREBLINKA CAMP

Treblinka was built to the northeast of Warsaw, and was set up on 23 July 1942. Although the first concentration camps were not meant to kill anyone, Treblinka was specifically designed for death.

By August 1941, over 70,000 handicapped German men, women, and children had been exterminated through Aktion T4, an operation to eliminate the weak. And the knowledge gained from that was used at Treblinka. Jews and Gypsies were worked at Treblinka I. When they died, they were disposed of at Treblinka II.

Some 700,000 to 900,000 Jews and about 2,000 Gypsies were killed here, the second highest casualty rate after Auschwitz-Birkenau.

BEŁŻEC CAMP

Bełżec was opened on 17 March 1942 specifically to exterminate the Jews and to "Germanize" the area as part of Nazi colonial expansion into Poland. As such, many non-Jewish Poles and Gypsies in the region were also sent here to die.

As early as April 1940, German Jews were in Bełżec as slave labor to prepare for the German invasion of Russia. In October 1941, however, Himmler gave the order to exterminate the Jews and Poles in order to make room for German Christian immigrants.

It's estimated that some 500,000 to 600,000 Jews, Poles, Russians, and Gypsies died here.

MAJDANEK CAMP

Majdanek was built to house 25,000 POWs in anticipation of Germany's invasion of Russia. But after the First Battle of Kiev in September 1941, there were over 50,000 Soviet POWs, so the camp was redesigned in October.

By December, there were 150,000 inmates and in March the following year, there were over 250,000. Originally meant to be a working camp, the authorities couldn't cope with the numbers, so it was turned into a labor and extermination facility. "Unhealthy" Germans were also sent here to die.

By 1945, 360,000 people were killed, including thousands of Germans unwanted by their own government.

CHEŁMNO CAMP

With no trains to Chełmno, prisoners were taken by truck or had to walk. Most abandoned their belongings along the way

Chelmno opened in December 1941 as part of Operation Reinhard to purge the Polish Jews from the Łódź Ghetto. To "Germanize" the area, the local, non-Jewish Poles were also sent here to die. As Germany expanded, other Jews and Gypsies from Austria, Bohemia, Germany, Hungary, Luxemburg, and Moravia were also put here.

Though primarily a death camp, it was also used for medical experimentation. It was here that doctors developed the mobile gas vans used in Operation Barbarossa against Russia to kill large numbers in open air.

The Polish government claims that about 340,000 people died in this camp, alone.

SOBIBÓR CAMP

Sobibor was built near the Polish town of Wlodawa in March 1942 to supplement the Bełżec camp which housed Jews deported from the Lublin Ghetto. It was at Sobibór that early experiments on gassing were carried out on several Jewish prisoners.

The fit and the unfit were first separated of those brought in. The latter were gassed immediately upon arrival, while the former were first worked to exhaustion. On 14 October 1943, the prisoners rose up in revolt and about 50 escaped, after which the authorities obliterated the camp.

Some 250,000 people died at the site, which is now gone, but a memorial center has been built there.

DACHAU CAMP

Dachau was built near Munich in 1933. Its first prisoners were Germans who opposed the Nazi regime, while its last inmates were SS officers awaiting trial in 1945. In 1935, its first minorities were Jehovah's Witnesses, followed by Germans of mixed descent, and immigrants.

Jews were sent here in August 1940. To accommodate more people, almost 100 other sub-camps were created throughout southern Germany and Austria, which were administered from Dachau. After the war, Germans expelled from Eastern Europe were kept here as they awaited resettlement.

It's believed that more than 243,000 died here by the time it was liberated in 1945.

MAUTHAUSEN-GUSEN CAMP

Stone gate topped with a large metal eagle holding a swastika; through the gate a building with two garage doors is visible

Mauthausen was built in upper Austria in August 1938, and was one of the first massive concentration camp complexes in Nazi Germany, and the last to be liberated by the Allies. The two main camps, Mauthausen and Gusen I, were labelled as "Grade III" camps, which meant that they were intended to be the toughest camps for the "Incorrigible political enemies of the Reich". Unlike many other concentration camps, which were intended for all categories of prisoners, Mauthausen was mostly used for extermination through labour of the intelligentsia – educated people and members of the higher social classes in occupied countries.

It is estimated that between 122.766 and 320.000 people were murdered in Mauthausen.

BERGEN-BELSEN CAMP

Female inmates at Bergen-Belsen after liberation in April 1945. They're collecting extra bread rations provided by the Allies

Female inmates at Bergen-Belsen after liberation in April 1945. They're collecting extra bread rations provided by the Allies

Bergen-Belsen in Germany's Lower-Saxony, was built in 1943 to be a POW camp. At its height, 95,000 international prisoners were kept here, requiring constant expansion throughout the war. Prominent Jewish hostages were also sent to this camp to exchange them for German POWs, so it was never meant to become an extermination facility.

Due to food and medical shortages, however, as well as unsanitary conditions and inadequate facilities, many died from starvation, disease, and lack of adequate care. When the Allies liberated it in 1945, they found some 13,000 corpses lying about.

It's estimated that at least 50,000 people died here.

BUCHENWALD CAMP

Buchenwald means beech forest, belying its horror, and was the first camp to be liberated by the western allies in WWII. Set up in July 1937, it was the also first camp built in Weimar, Germany, as well as the largest after Dachau.

Created for Communists, Freemasons, Gypsies, Jehovah's Witnesses, Jews, Poles, Soviets, Slavs, homosexuals, and common criminals, it began life as a working prison for arms production. But in 1942, they began medical experimentation on the inmates. In August 1944, an Allied bombing raid hit the facility, killing 388 and wounding some 2,000.

By 1945, 33,462 had died from executions, malnutrition, and experimentation.

CONCLUSION

Extermination camp Aushwitz, today one of the symbols of the Second World War, and the Holocaust, was the biggest camp of the kind in the entire Third Reich. Beginning in 1942 altogether with numerous subcamps, it functioned as both concentration, and extermination camp. During its operation, approximately 1,3 million people were brought there, and about one million died in gas chambers, due to hunger, due to work under inhumane conditions, or as a result of pseudo-medical experiments which were a part of Third Reich policy.

Kulmhof in Chełmno nad Nerem, built by the Third Reich in December 1941, was the second extermination camp located in Poland. Initially, Jewish population from Kraj Warty (Reichsgau Wartheland) and prisoners who came from Western Europe were brought there, and exterminated. After ghetto in Łódź had been done away with, its population was also brought to Kulmhof, and exterminated. Approximately 160.000 people perished in trucks called "gas vans", which were trucks equipped with gas chambers.

In the area of The General Government there were four german extermination camps, where between 1942 and 1943 about two million people were murdered, mainly under Operation Reinhardt (English term for Aktion Reinhardt). Its main goal was to exterminate Jewish population on Polish soil. The operation was carried out by Guard Forces of the SS in Lublin.

In the camp in Bełżec, built in 1942, Germans exterminated victims by means of chambers with exhaust gas. At least 434.506 people perished there. Camp in Sobibór, which was done away with in November 1943 after an uprising organised by prisoners, brought death to about 250.000 people. Within the site of the extermination camp in Treblinka, also done away with in 1943, 800.000 Jews were murdered. In the meantime mass exterminations under Operation Reinhardt also took place in the camp in Majdanek, however, number of victims is unknown.

All the concentration, labor, and extermination camps which functioned during the Second World War on Polish soil annexed by Germany, and in the area of The General Government were initiated by German authorities. Camps were administered by German functionaries. Camps were used to carry out bestial directives issued by the authorities of The Third

Reich, including slave work, and pseudo-medical experiments..

Disclaimer

This book is not intended as a tool for terrorism neither is it written to open up healed wounds of the past, this book is only written to provide the reader with polish and accurate history on german camps in Poland during world war 2.

(history, education)

ABOUT THE AUTHOR

MY NAME IS Piotr Lewicki. I am a PhD holder in history

I come from Poland and I wanted show you true history about German Death Camps in Poland.

Yes !!! Death Camps in Poland were German not Polish. Media are trying blur the real facts and that was my inspiration to write this book.

Millions of people has been killed in German Camps including my grandparents so each person which lost his life in German Death Camps during World War 2 deserve to world know the truth.

Do not go yet; One last thing to do

If you enjoyed this book or found it useful I'd be very grateful if you'd post a short review on it. Your support really does make a difference and I read all the reviews personally so I can get your feedback and make this book even better.

Thanks again for your support!

Made in the USA
Monee, IL
10 April 2021